T0329253

THE TENURE OF
AGRICULTURAL LAND

THE TENURE OF
AGRICULTURAL LAND

BY

C. S. ORWIN, M.A.

AND

W. R. PEEL, M.A., D.S.O.

SECOND EDITION

CAMBRIDGE

AT THE UNIVERSITY PRESS

1926

Our heavenly Father hath not judged it right
To leave the road of agriculture light:
'Twas he who first made husbandry a plan,
And care a whetstone for the wit of man;
Nor suffers he his own domains to lie
Asleep in cumbrous old-world lethargy.

Georgics, I. 140–145
tr. R. D. BLACKMORE

CAMBRIDGE
UNIVERSITY PRESS

University Printing House, Cambridge CB2 8BS, United Kingdom

Cambridge University Press is part of the University of Cambridge.

It furthers the University's mission by disseminating knowledge in the pursuit of education, learning and research at the highest international levels of excellence.

www.cambridge.org
Information on this title: www.cambridge.org/9781316509586

© Cambridge University Press 1926

First published July 1925
Second edition January 1926
First paperback edition 2015

A catalogue record for this publication is available from the British Library

ISBN 978-1-316-50958-6 Paperback

PREFACE
TO SECOND EDITION

THE speedy exhaustion of the first issue of this little study of the present position of land tenure and the outlook for it, is evidence of widespread interest in the problem of the development of the country-side. Advocacy of the expropriation of the landlord and State ownership of the land is difficult, in view of the prejudice which associated ideas have created, and it is gratifying to be able to record that both reviewers and correspondents (with only a single exception) have recognised that the proposals contained in the following pages represent a *bona fide* effort, free from all political intent, to find a means of arresting the decay of the agricultural industry of this country. A *Times* reviewer has reminded us that so long ago as 1912 Lord Ernle pointed out that to say that landlords were too impoverished to make the required expenditure for the equipment, maintenance and improvement of their farms was equivalent to saying that "the modern system of farming had broken down in one of its most essential features[1]." The break-up of the old estates, following

[1] The *Times*, 1st September, 1925.

the war, has proved the truth of this conclusion, and that the new conditions which farmers have perforce evolved are unlikely to bring about any amelioration of the position has recently been foretold by Lord Ernle's present successor at the Ministry of Agriculture.

With the diagnosis of the case made with such authority we respectfully and most fully agree. In the following pages we indicate the treatment which we would recommend, and it remains for those who do not like it to suggest a better one. A few corrections and additions have been made, and a paragraph is included by way of comment on certain aspects of the proposals of the Liberal Land Committee, whose report has just been published; otherwise we have found no reason for departing from anything contained in the first issue.

C. S. O.
W. R. P.

AGRICULTURAL ECONOMICS
RESEARCH INSTITUTE,
OXFORD.

October, 1925.

PREFACE

TO FIRST EDITION

THE RT HON. EDWARD WOOD, M.P., spoke on
9 December, 1924, as follows:

"As I conceive it, at the present time, taking a view of
British agriculture that is not confined to this year, or to
next year, there is something like a silent revolution in
progress within its borders. We are, unless I mistake,
witnessing in England the gradual disappearance of the old
landowning class. Within the last five years the number of
occupying owners has almost exactly doubled, and at the
present time those occupying owners hold something like
25 per cent. of the total area under crops and grass. For my
part, I am very glad to see the principle of ownership
extended, because I think that it is the sheet anchor of the
country. But we ought not to shut our eyes to the fact that,
as that process goes on, it is raising a problem that is likely
to become increasingly acute, and that is the problem of
finding the maintenance capital of the land as apart from
the current working capital. Any of us who are accustomed
to live in the country, who watch this process going on, see
to-day a deterioration in what I may call the capital equipment of the land and the soil, whether in building or in
drainage. I could go on indefinitely through the category
in which we see that process at work....The real truth of
the matter is that the old landowner did supply the essential
capital equipment of the land at a most astonishingly cheap
rate of interest. If that class, by taxation or for one reason

or another, is gradually disappearing, what is going to happen?...The new owners who survive will find their position increasingly difficult—and many a new occupying owner who has, in many cases, sunk too much of his capital on that side of the business, has left himself inadequate capital with which to run his ordinary working business. That means either that the soil is going to be starved and is gradually going to lose some of its fecundity by the land becoming waterlogged and so on; or the nation is going to say: 'We cannot watch this process going on,' and the State will come in to fill the function of the old landlord by lending capital. When it does that you may depend upon it that it will claim some measure of control in the business that it finances, and so you may well find yourselves in the course of the next thirty or forty years within measurable distance of something like nationalisation by a side wind."

The proposals for the reconstruction of land tenure contained in the following pages relate only to rural England. In effect they may be found to contain little of novelty; even before the days of Mill and of Henry George there were individuals and groups of persons who have advocated the abolition of private property in land. Most of them have been identified closely with the more revolutionary elements of the most advanced political party, and inevitably their proposals have been launched on a sea of prejudice which has prevented them from reaching a haven of calm consideration; some, indeed, have never merited any such consideration of their views by reason of their frankly confiscatory nature, which is never likely to make any appeal to the public conscience. Since the

breakdown of Mr Lloyd George's Land Valuation less
has been heard of the need for land reform upon such
lines, but the recent election has shown that there are
still those who think that a prosperous countryside can
arise only from the ashes of the landlord's home and
from "the destruction of the last vestiges of feudalism"
whatever this phrase may mean.

The authors have no political ends to serve; they
know that under the system of tenure which these
reformers are so ready to condemn England has attained
to a standard of efficiency in farming which has been
an example to the world; they have seen so much of
the advantages to many a rural community of the
leadership of a benevolent despot as to enable them to
assess at its true value much of the criticism that s
levelled against him. But the old order, with all its
merits, is giving place to new. The transfer of land was
immensely stimulated by the Finance Act (1909–10),
1910, and continued to gain impetus until the slump in
values consequent on the deflation policy following the
conclusion of Peace. There are again signs of increasing
activity in the land-market; once more the land-
speculator is raising his ugly head, and with the probability of some five years of stable government under
an administration not avowedly hostile to the landlord,
coupled with the uncertainty of the position thereafter,
it seems reasonable to suppose that the break-up of
the old estates will proceed at a greater and a greater
rate.

In these circumstances it behoves everyone who has

the interests of rural life and labour at heart to think whether there is no alternative to the policy of drift, and to give unbiassed consideration to any serious counter proposals. Amongst these the question of State ownership of land (which has nothing whatever to do with State control of agriculture) comes foremost to the mind, and in the following pages the attempt is made to give it dispassionate consideration as a great economic problem having no necessary connection with the aims and objects of any one of the political parties of the State.

C. S. O.
W. R. P.

AGRICULTURAL ECONOMICS
RESEARCH INSTITUTE,
OXFORD.
January, 1925.

CONTENTS

CHAPTER I

INTRODUCTORY

THE trend of modern land legislation has been to restrict the scope of the landlord as a director of farming enterprise, and to reduce him, step by step, more nearly to the state of a mere receiver of rent. No criticism is necessarily implied in this assertion, which is nothing more than a summary of the facts. The earliest Agricultural Holdings Act, that of 1875, did little more than give the authority of statute law to that which was already customary on many estates; moreover it contained a contracting-out clause. The Acts of 1883 and 1900 were, in the main, the natural development of the principles upon which the first Act was based, embodying the results of further experience, and eliminating the contracting-out clause. The Act of 1906[1] was mainly of the same character, but it also marks a considerable step in the direction of the elimination of the landlord's control in two particulars. In the first place, it voided all covenants in agricultural leases and agreements and any custom of the country restrictive of the tenant's freedom of cropping[2]. The conception of such covenants was the preservation of the fertility of the soil and fundamentally they were sound; they indicated to the tenant the best practice of the locality, based upon the wider experience of the

[1] Introduced as the Land Tenure Bill and repealed, before coming into operation, by a consolidating act, the Agricultural Holdings Act, 1908.
[2] See *Agricultural Holdings Act*, 1908, sec. 26.

landlord and his advisers. But it must be admitted that in many cases the time had come when they were apt to lag behind established practice, and since the days when science had begun to place new means for the control of soil fertility in the hands of the farmer, they had become obsolete at the best, and at the worst a bar to progress.

In the second place, the Act of 1906 took away from the agricultural landlord the right which all landlords had possessed up to that date, and which all of them other than agricultural landowners still enjoy, of re-possessing themselves of their property, after due notice, without compensation to the tenant for the disturbance suffered by him. Unless the landlord could show "good and sufficient cause" for terminating a tenancy, or for refusing to renew a lease, he was rendered liable to compensate the tenant "for the loss or expense directly attributable to his quitting his holding[1]." This was a step definitely in the direction of the dual ownership of the land.

The Act of 1913 was unimportant in the present connection, and, passing over the emergency legislation of the War period, the next enactment limiting the freedom of the landlord was the Agriculture Act, 1920. This measure was, in part, the outcome of the recommendations contained in a Majority[2] Report of the Royal Commission on Agriculture of 1919, but as regards the position of the landlord it travelled far beyond the findings of the Commission. In the first place, it defined with greater precision the conditions under which a tenant could obtain compensation from his landlord for disturbance in his tenancy, and laid

[1] See *Agricultural Holdings Act*, 1908, sec. 11.   [2] A majority of *one*.

down the amount of the compensation recoverable[1]. Experience had shown that the disturbance clause in the Act of 1906 was inoperative in practice, and did nothing to meet the farmers' demand for security of tenure; the later enactment seems to have met the difficulty, and it is now almost impossible to remove a tenant for any reason except bad farming.

In the second place, the Act of 1920 gave the tenant the right to demand an arbitration upon the amount of his rent; and if this demand were refused by the landlord and the tenant should give notice and quit his holding in consequence, he became entitled to compensation for disturbance "in the same manner as if the tenancy had been terminated by notice to quit given by the landlord[2]." This is a step in the direction of the establishment of a Rent Court.

In the third place, the Agriculture Act provided for the administration of the landlord's estate by a Receiver and Manager appointed by the Minister of Agriculture if such a step appeared to him, after consultation with the Agricultural Committee, necessary or desirable in the national interest in those cases where the estate, or any part of it, was grossly mismanaged "to such an extent as to prejudice materially the production of food thereon or the welfare of those who are engaged in the cultivation of the estate." For reasons in no way connected with this clause it was repealed by the Corn Production Acts (Repeal) Act, 1921, before an occasion had arisen for the exercise by the Minister of the powers thus conferred upon him, and they have not been re-enacted in subsequent legislation. The fact that he was vested even though only for a short time with such

---

[1] Sec. 10, sub-sec. 6.   [2] *Ibid.* sub-sec. 3.

powers is of considerable importance as being another link in the chain by which modern legislation seeks more and more to restrict the scope of the landlord and to substitute Public Authority as the active participator in the development of rural industry.

There is, however, another and a far more potent force at work in this direction. The ownership of broad acres has never been so lucrative as many imagine it to be, nor as a glance at the rent-roll of an estate might suggest. Even prior to the War the expenses of management and maintenance accounted for £30 out of every £100 of rent received[1] and the proportion has risen considerably since. The surplus, whatever it may be, is subject, very frequently, to charges of all kinds— mortgages, jointures, improvement rent-charges, etc.— about which the public hears nothing, and cases are not unknown in which payments such as these have absorbed practically the whole of the surplus from an apparently extensive estate. But, even in the more normal case, the net income is rarely available for the landowner to the extent that the incomes of other classes of investors are, for the owners of agricultural property have behind them a tradition of sharing their possessions with the community in which they live to an extent unknown of any other class. Theorists may animadvert upon the amount of unproductive labour involved in the upkeep of a country mansion and the life that it stands for; they may talk of the pauperisation of the people through the patronage of local institutions by the squire; but the fact remains that these things were big factors in rural social life. The reduction of

[1] From an inquiry made in the year 1909. See *Journal of the Land Agents' Society*, vol. III, pp. 214–219 (1909).

spending power consequent on the War has now completed what the Agricultural Depression began, and what Sir William Harcourt's death duties continued[1], and for many landlords the breaking-point has been reached. They cannot carry on, and it is just these conditions which are so favourable to the development of that parasite on agriculture, the land-speculator. The landowner is offered a fair price to clear out in one transaction, the speculator knowing that he has means at his command, to which the other will not resort, which will enable him to recoup himself, and leave a handsome profit into the bargain, when he comes to negotiate for the break-up of the estate amongst the tenants upon it. Thus it is that farmers are compelled, not only to buy holdings they would prefer to rent, but, to pay unduly for them in the fear of losing their homes and means of livelihood; very often they must find ways to finance the purchase, and "there is no worse landlord than borrowed money." Thus it is that timber speculators are able to acquire woodlands, and, erecting temporary saw-mills, to proceed to lay them waste, afterwards selling the devastated freehold for what it will fetch. In a subsequent chapter figures will be found indicating the extent of this process, and there are signs that it will be accelerated rather than retarded in coming years. As regards the farmer, he is always obliged to buy at a price which combines an assessment of his necessity for retaining a home and a means of livelihood with the ordinary commercial value of the land; and when it is remembered that the process of dismemberment of estates is most active in a rising market for

[1] Estate Duty was first levied on land by Sir William Harcourt's Finance Act of 1894.

commodities, it is obvious that he may pay a sum far beyond that which will allow him a fair return on his outlay when times again become normal. Proof of this is afforded by the enactment of a measure in 1923 designed to assist those who were compelled to buy their holdings during the brief period of high prices following the termination of the War[1].

As regards rural society generally, the disappearance of the landowner deprives it of its natural focus. With the dispersal of his property and the sale of his home nothing remains to tie the squire to the locality in which he has exercised for so long, in greater or less degree, functions of leadership and wise control. At the present time hundreds of country houses, once the centres of an active social life, are in the market for disposal, whilst others have been acquired for sanatoria, schools, religious houses, asylums and similar purposes. It may be that this is their best use in the changing circumstances of the times, and that eventually a new social order will arise in the countryside in which its more stately homes will have no place; but many people do not realise the extent of the collapse in rural society which is the first result of their abandonment, bringing discomfort and even misery to many of their more humble neighbours. Indeed, there are some who think that it is not for the good of rural society that the landlord element should be eliminated from it by the uncontrolled operation of economic pressure. The greatest single cause of social unrest is the segregation of classes. Where everything is understood, everything is forgiven, and people can only understand each other when they have opportunities of mixing freely one with

---

[1] *The Agricultural Credits Act*, 1923, sec. 1.

another; on the estate and the farm, at work and at play, all classes of society on the land are in almost daily contact. The degree of intimacy is, of course, variable, but at least the component classes of the rural community are familiar with each other's mode of life, and with that comes a clearer comprehension of the humanity common to all classes. Under industrialism in its modern organisation these conditions have ceased, almost entirely, to prevail; great groups of men, brought together by reason of their employment, have no personal contact of any kind with those by whom they are employed, for the days have passed when the factory-owner lived amongst his workers and was a real personality to them. The rural workers of England represent practically the largest industry of the country, and the only one in which industrial strife is practically unknown. This is not due to the rate of wages, for they are the lowest in the country; nor is it due to the amenities of rural life, for these, as popularly understood, are largely absent. It is due in no small measure to the better comprehension of class by class, and rural society can suffer nothing but loss by the elimination of its principal co-ordinating element and rallying point, the landlord, who seems likely to disappear unless some means can be devised which will enable him to continue to function as an essential factor of it whilst relieving him, at the same time, of the impossible financial burden which the ownership of broad acres has become.

Does not the acquisition of the land by the State offer the only way of escape from the position into which the country is drifting? Assured of a square deal, the landlord might be expected gladly to exchange the incubus of land for a gilt-edged security, whilst at the same time retaining his interest in his home and in his neighbours, being free to apply himself to local administration and the needs of local society without the creeping paralysis induced by financial stress. The farmer, instead of being reduced to fighting an unconscionable speculator with one hand tied behind his back, would welcome the alternative of continuing as tenant at a fair rent, and free to apply the whole of his capital to the management of his farm.

On these grounds alone there appears to be a strong *prima facie* case for a direction of current events by the State. There is, however, another consideration of importance arising in connection with the private ownership of land. At the present time no sane person would advocate the protection of the agricultural industry by the State, but it is by no means absurd to suggest that circumstances might arise under which the community would be prepared to pay a price to secure a larger amount of agriculture. It might be thought necessary to take steps to maintain or to improve the standard of living on the land; to provide for the absorption of a larger proportion of the population in rural industry; to secure certain forms of husbandry normally uneconomic. But a condition precedent to such a course would be that the price required should be paid to the persons most actively concerned in agricultural production, both farmers and land-workers, and not to their indirect partners, the owners of the soil. For there is no answer to the argument that any benefit to the land will accrue, sooner or later, to the landlord. Rent is paid on a fixed contract, and time was when an age-long tradition forbade raising the rent of a sitting tenant; but war-time conditions broke through this tradition, and post-war

legislation has provided machinery for varying con-
tracts[1]. An all-round improvement in farming fortune
produces a competition for farms which results, inevitably, in passing on some measure of the value of
this improvement to the landlord; how much of it
passes to him, and how soon, will vary in different cases,
but it is a question only of time and of degree. Under
the unfettered operation of economic forces no one but
the most prejudiced would grudge this participation
by the landlord in the ups as well as in the downs of
fortune, but should circumstances arise which call for
interference with the normal course of events in the
interests of the community at large, the State will
always be precluded from taking direct action to foster
rural industry so long as private property in land exists
in conjunction with the system of tenant-occupation.

It is not suggested that Government during the
past forty years has been concerned only with legislation
tending to reduce the landlord's status and to increase
that of the tenant; nor that the fact that any benefits to
agriculture tend in the long run to be absorbed in rent
has imposed a check on what the country has been
prepared to do for the farming industry. It is not
necessary to set out here all that has been done or
attempted during the past generation, for the measures
taken by successive administrations since the close of
the War are a sufficient indication of the national concern in the prosperity of agriculture. Probably the
most beneficial action taken by the State is that of
the reorganisation of agricultural education and research, for whenever problems more immediately
pressing have been tackled the results of Government

---

[1] *Vide* the *Agricultural Holdings Act*, 1923, sec. 13, sub-sec. 3.

action have been almost entirely negative. In 1919 Mr Lloyd George's Coalition Government appointed a Royal Commission "to inquire into the economic prospects of the agricultural industry in Great Britain, with special reference to the adjustment of a balance between the prices of agricultural commodities, the costs of production, the remuneration of labour, and hours of employment." The members of this Commission were so sharply divided that ultimately they dispersed without producing a Final Report, but an Interim Report led to the placing on the Statute Book, in 1920, of an Act of a character unknown since the days of the Corn Laws, the Agriculture Act of that year, by which the growers of wheat and oats were to be subsidised whenever their industry proved unprofitable. That state of affairs which this measure was framed to remedy arose at once, but before the day of reckoning arrived the very administration responsible for passing the Act through Parliament had induced the same House to repeal it.

Another Act resulting from the report of a Departmental Committee was the Agricultural Credits Act, 1923. Its objects are to assist landowners with credit for estate improvements; to provide short-term loans for farmers; and to supply mortgage credit to owner-occupiers who bought their holdings during the land boom following the War. The only conclusion to be drawn from the operation of the Act is that the urgency of the demand for credit had been over-estimated, or else that the means provided under the Act to meet it are unsuited to the needs of the persons most concerned.

In 1922 further investigations into the state of agriculture were set on foot, one, a general inquiry "into

the methods which have been adopted in other countries during the last fifty years to increase the prosperity
of agriculture and to secure the fullest possible use of
the land for the production of food and the employment
of labour at a living wage, and to advise as to the methods
by which those results can be achieved in this country,"
which was carried out by the Agricultural Tribunal of
Investigation; the other, a particular inquiry "into the
methods and costs of selling and distributing agricultural, horticultural and dairy produce in Great Britain,
and to consider whether, and, if so, by what means the
disparity between the price received by the producer
and that paid by the consumer can be diminished,"
conducted by a Departmental Committee under the
Chairmanship of the Earl of Linlithgow. And a number
of other investigations into matters of greater or less
importance to the agricultural industry have been
made without much consequent action.

Many specifics for the improvement of the state of
rural industry are on offer, both in the reports of the
foregoing bodies and in the writings and utterances of
many friends of agriculture. The attractive labels of
some of them are hardly justified by their contents;
others, again, more promising as amelioratives, are of
their nature slow in action. There are many advocates,
for example, of the closer settlement of the land by the
multiplication of small holdings, and certainly a reversion to a greater proportion of family-farming would
increase both the population on the land and the gross
product, though whether the surplus available for con-
sumption by the industrial classes would be increased
is much less certain. Nor must it be forgotten that
although the small holding may open a road to advance-

ment for the few it entails a life of greater toil in exchange for an incommensurate reward to the many, and human happiness is measured less by what the individual may have of material wealth than by what his neighbours enjoy. Thus, although many Continental countries maintain altogether, or over large districts, a contented peasant population, it cannot be argued that such a condition is capable of reproduction in this country where the comparison between the material wealth of rural and urban workers is so much more easily made. Fifteen years of the artificial creation of small holdings by the State have not sufficed to stay the decline in their total number.

Almost all students of rural economics are agreed that the organisation of the industry on a co-operative basis, both for the supply of requisites and for the distribution of products, would result in greatly increased efficiency. Without looking abroad, the success of the achievement in Ireland, partial and local though it be, is an indication of what may be expected from the spread of co-operation in this country, but it is generally recognised that organisation on this basis for the home market is a matter of far greater difficulty than in countries organising almost exclusively for an export trade; consequently its extension in any large degree must be a matter of considerable time.

A small but enthusiastic group of those engaged in the study of rural problems maintains that it is our system of tenant-occupation that is at fault, and that the great need of the country is for a much larger proportion of occupying-owners—"it is the magic of ownership which turns sand into gold." Certainly, here and there men may be found who feel a degree of insecurity as tenants which militates against the fullest use and development of their land, but these are the exceptions. Recent legislation has removed all reasonable grounds of apprehension on the score of insecurity[1], and if there is one thing upon which nearly all farmers in this country agree it is that a bad landlord is better than none; they have never indicated the smallest desire for a Land Purchase Act on the lines of the Wyndham Act, admirable though it may have been in relation to the conditions of land tenure in Ireland in 1903.

The Report of the Haversham Committee[2] leaves no room for doubt on this point.

"The evidence we have heard makes it quite clear that tenants do not desire to purchase their farms except as an alternative to leaving altogether." (Sec. 76.)

"Of the farmers who gave evidence before us, only three advocated purchase save as an absolute necessity. One land agent stated that, putting himself in a tenant's position, nothing would induce him to buy; another was of opinion that no tenant desired to purchase except under compulsion." (Sec. 77.)

"In the same way the experience of all County Councils since the Small Holdings Allotments Act, 1908 came into force shows that the great desire of the applicants is to rent land; in fact, only 2 per cent. desired to acquire it." (Sec. 81.)

In view of this evidence the Committee found itself forced

"to fall back on some system which will protect the tenant against dispossession, whilst at the same time securing to the occupier all the advantages now enjoyed on well managed estates. This, in our opinion, can be secured by the acquisition and management of landed estates by the State." (Sec. 83.)

[1] See *Agricultural Holdings Act*, 1923, sec. 12.
[2] Report of the Departmental Committee appointed to inquire into the position of Tenant Farmers on the occasion of any Change in the Ownership of their Holdings, etc. Cd. 6030 (1912).

It should, perhaps, be stated that the recommendation as to State Purchase was not unanimous, five of the twelve members of the Committee dissenting from it.

There are many other measures of reform and reconstruction, from afforestation to apiculture, all of which have their advocates, but they need not be particularised here. Like the foregoing nearly all of them are concerned mainly with the farmer and his business, though they have as their ultimate object the increase of production from the land and the maintenance of rural society. It is not intended to attempt to assess either their intrinsic value or their economic importance; in the long run the cost of production in England in relation to prices in the world market will determine the changes in the character of rural industry in this country, and all the reforms proposed will not suffice to bring about the breaking of a single additional acre nor the employment of one extra man except in so far as it be profitable so to do. What is intended here is not the study of farm organisation problems but the prior consideration of the problems presented by the ownership of the land itself. Not everyone realises as yet the great changes which have swept over large parts of the country in recent years, bringing in their train a new social order, the ultimate effects of which cannot yet be foretold. It is not too early, however, to give them careful consideration, in so far as they are already revealed, with the object of making some assessment of their effect on the life of the community; and further, of determining whether the time may not be near when some control or direction of the process now undermining the ancient structure of English rural society should be required of the State.

CHAPTER II

THE DISTRIBUTION OF OWNERSHIP

THE cultivated area of England and Wales extends to 25,755,000 acres, besides which there are 5,028,000 acres of rough grazings and 1,085,000 acres of waste[1]. No accurate statement of the division of this area amongst public and private owners is possible, but the extent of land already publicly or semi-publicly owned is very considerable. Thus, the Crown property in charge of the Commissioners of Woods and Forests, that is to say, property devoted to revenue purposes, includes agricultural land as follows:

135,000 acres agricultural land;
  72,000 acres woodlands;
125,000 acres unenclosed wastes subject to common rights.

The land belonging to, and administered by, the Duchy of Lancaster extends to 18,000 acres, distributed over nine counties.

The Duchy of Cornwall owns and administers very considerable estates in land, the area extending approximately to 133,400 acres, situated mainly in the Counties of Devon, Somerset and Cornwall, but included in this total are 80,000 acres on Dartmoor, besides a considerable extent of waste and woodland in Cornwall.

The Ecclesiastical Commissioners administer about 240,000 acres distributed very widely throughout the country.

The Universities of Oxford and Cambridge are the

[1] *Agricultural Statistics*, 1925.

owners of broad acres, though not to the extent that they once were. The most recent figures available are those for 1918[1] in which year the areas under University and College control were:

Oxford	175,856	acres
Cambridge	115,527	,,
Total	291,383	,,

Separate figures for each College are not available, nor are they important in this connection. It is generally reported, however, that considerable sales were effected by some during recent years.

Other charities are large landowners, in the aggregate; not only do the endowments of schools, hospitals, etc., take, frequently, the form of land, but also in very many parishes of England, lands are held by charitable trusts of one kind or another, the revenues to be applied to objects specified. No return of the total extent of such property appears to have been made, nor would it be possible closely to estimate it.

There is still another and a growing class of public landowners, namely the County Councils. Under the Small Holdings Act, 1908, the County Councils were empowered to acquire land, either by purchase or by lease, and compulsorily if not otherwise obtainable, for the purpose of the closer settlement of the land. No doubt most of its supporters acted from a firm belief in the economic advantages of the small unit of farming, drawing conclusions, often fallacious, from the predominance of the peasant farmer in other countries, but the measure appealed to not a few people as being, in

[1] *Report of the Royal Commission on Oxford and Cambridge Universities*, 1922. Appendices, pp. 356–7 and 364–5.

effect, an act to abolish private ownership in land. "I am not particularly interested in the multiplication of small holdings," said the Chairman of the Small Holdings Committee, set up in one of the larger counties under this Act, "my interest arises from the fact that this is the first step towards the nationalisation of the land." This aspect of the Small Holdings Act is indisputable, and had there been a really effective demand for land by small farmers, sixteen years of the operation of the Act might have witnessed a very considerable transference of land into public ownership. Events have proved, however, that the rate of creation of small holdings by the County Councils has been slower than the absorption of the already existing small farms. However, even so, a considerable acreage in the aggregate is now administered by the County Councils; at the end of November, 1924, 384,052 acres were in the possession of the English Counties, the amount ranging from 27,861 acres held by Norfolk, and 26,257 acres held by Somerset, down to 219 acres held by Westmorland. Of the total area administered by the English Counties under this Act, almost exactly four-fifths (307,906 acres) is the property of the counties, the other fifth (76,146 acres) being held by them on lease. The figures for the Welsh Counties add some 58,000 acres to the total area administered under the Act, making about 442,000 acres in England and Wales.

From the foregoing figures, incomplete as they must necessarily be, it is evident that a very large acreage of land is already in public, or semi-public, ownership, and it is no more than true to say that its administration by the public bodies and charitable trusts who own it is as effective as that of the average privately-owned estate.

There is, however, another and a rapidly growing class of landowners, whose growth, indeed, has prompted this essay, namely the owner-occupier. The owner-occupier, whether large or small, has never been an important factor in English rural society until now; the tenancy system has predominated at all stages of the history of the agricultural industry. Of recent years, however, the number of those owning the holdings they occupy has increased something like a hundred per cent., and this increase is associated directly with the break-up of the old family estates in the circumstances already detailed. The process was immensely stimulated by the passing of the Finance Act (1909–10), 1910, after its rejection, once, by the House of Lords, and by the campaign against the landlords which preceded its introduction. Further, agricultural prices had been improving since 1908; the gain was not spectacular, but the tendency was definitely upwards, as is shown by the movements in the Agricultural Index Number[1] for the principal commodities:

Index Number of Prices of Produce sold off Farms in England and Wales.

Year	Index Number
1906–8	100
1909	99
1910	104
1911	106
1912	112
1913	112
1914	111

[1] The Agricultural Index Number is an approximate measure of the extent to which the variations in price, from year to year, affect the receipts by farmers from the sale of their produce.

The only way in which the landlord could participate in this improvement was by raising his tenants' rents, and this was a course contrary to all his traditions.

These circumstances, partly political, more largely economic, combined to suggest the policy of sale. No record exists, nor could it now be compiled, of the transactions in land in the years immediately following Mr Lloyd George's famous Budget, but figures furnished by the Estate Exchange, in Tokenhouse Yard, E.C., of sales registered there serve as an index to the trend of events, though, of course, they are valueless as a record of the total transactions in land:

Acreage of Agricultural Land in England and Wales Registered at the Estate Exchange, London, as being sold during the years 1908–12[1].

Year	Acreage
1908	97,263
1909	100,273
1910	114,661
1911	188,009
1912	192,624

These figures, incomplete though they are, indicate very clearly that transactions in land had doubled themselves in a period of about five years. It is common knowledge that in many cases the tenants were the buyers. "They greatly preferred to remain undisturbed as tenants. Many could not spare the capital to buy. But what was the position? During the period of the greatest activity in the sales of estates there have been very few farms to let. The sitting tenant knew that it would be difficult to find another farm. He knew, too, that if he did not buy there would be no lack of other

[1] See T. E. Marks, *The Land and the Commonwealth*, p. 30

buyers. His experience of the land, added perhaps to that of previous generations of his family, had thoroughly taught him its capabilities. His staff of men, his herds and flocks were suited to the farm. Further, there was frequently a very strong personal and family attachment to the place. Times were improving. Capable men were making reasonable returns[1]." But whilst it is common knowledge that the tenants were buyers to a very large extent during this period of activity in the land market (1910–14) it is a remarkable fact that the acreage and the number of holdings of agricultural land officially returned as being occupied by the owners shows a marked decline:

Acreage and Number of Holdings of Agricultural Land owned by the Occupiers in England and Wales, 1910–14.

Year	Acres	Holdings
1910	3,329,015	55,433
1911	3,246,971	54,176
1912	2,954,491	50,972
1913	2,890,559	48,760
1914	2,961,979	49,204

Thus, while the returns of sales indicate an increase of something like 100 per cent. in the dealings in land, and while tenants were known to be purchasers in many cases, the official returns show a decline of about 12 per cent. in the acreage of land owned by the occupiers.

Soon after the collection of the *Statistics* for the year 1914 the War broke out, and for the next four years dealings in land were much less active, and the area in the occupation of the owners was practically stationary:

[1] *The Land Question*, II, Knight, Frank and Rutley, pp. 6–7.

Acreage and Number of Holdings of Agricultural Land owned by the Occupiers in England and Wales, 1915–18.

Year	Acres	Holdings
1915	3,092,302 ⎫	
1916	3,085,099 ⎬ No returns	
1917	3,018,314 ⎪	
1918	3,161,584 ⎭	

During this time, however, agricultural prices had continued the advance begun in 1910, until in 1918 they showed an increase over the basic period of 1906–8 of more than 250 per cent.:

Index Number of Prices of Produce sold off Farms in England and Wales.

Year	Index Number
1906–8	100
1915	138
1916	178
1917	214
1918	253

The farmer's costs had also increased but not in the same proportion, and whilst the landlord's costs for estate equipment and maintenance had advanced at the same rates as the farmer's, increases in rent, though fairly general, were nothing like commensurate with them.

Under these circumstances—the farmer on the crest of a wave of prosperity (which was to break far sooner than he generally anticipated) and the landlord called upon to incur increasing costs without a proportionately increasing revenue—it is not surprising that the cessation of hostilities should have been followed by the throwing of estates on the market all over the country[1], and by the purchase of their holdings by the occupants. No records exist of the extent of sales during the years 1919–24, but the fact that more than 3¼ million acres of land passed into the possession of their occupiers in this short period of time is indicative of the magnitude of the transactions:

Acreage and Number of Holdings of Agricultural Land owned by the Occupiers in England and Wales, 1919–24.

Year	Acres	Holdings
1919	3,296,452	48,665
1920	4,102,556	57,234
1921	5,231,847	70,469
1922	4,639,615	62,680
1923	6,273,109	87,894
1924	6,574,044[2]	94,236

The year 1922 makes a curious break in the series but the total result is very remarkable, showing, as it does, a doubling both of the acreage of land and of the number of holdings farmed by owner-occupiers in six short years.

Here is the proof of the "silent revolution" which, as the Minister of Agriculture said shortly after coming into office, is going on to-day in rural England—the passing of the great landowner, the birth of the farmer-owner. Both of these are the victims of economic pressure, for just as the squire cannot afford to stay so cannot his tenant afford to leave. "What is going to happen?" asks Mr Wood, and, answering his own question, he has put on record his belief that the new owners will not have the capital necessary for the maintenance of the permanent equipment of the land—

[1] There is some evidence that the tendency to sell was more pronounced in those counties predominantly arable.

[2] Equal to nearly one quarter of the cultivated area of the country.

capital that the old landlords have lent to rural industry at a philanthropic rate of interest—with the result that there will be a steady deterioration of the land until a point is reached at which the State will have to step in to supply the needed capital. "And so, within the next thirty or forty years we may find ourselves within a measurable distance of something like nationalisation by a side wind."

Those who know the country best will find no fault with the Minister's assessment of the position. The farmer has been used to take the largest farm that his capital, employed as working capital, would finance; he has been used to look to his landlord to perform the principal works of maintenance required to keep his holding in a productive condition. He has not the capital to buy the freehold and to do these things himself; and if he should have to borrow money to save his home he will have oftentimes to pay more for the use of it than it will earn. "There is no worse landlord than borrowed money." Can anyone doubt that in thirty or forty years the State may have to take a hand?

But why wait so long? If this process of transfer of land to a class insufficiently equipped with the means to develop it, or even to maintain it, is likely to continue, why should the State stand on one side and content itself with the contemplation of the steady deterioration of its greatest wealth-producing asset—almost the only one which produces wealth without consuming it? Why wait until irreparable damage has been done instead of stepping in to obviate it? Is it not the more statesman-like, the more truly conservative course, to act at once, and instead of saying—"We cannot watch this process going on," to say "We will not allow it even to begin"?

CHAPTER III

STATE PURCHASE

I. SOME OLD ALTERNATIVES

THE traditional argument in favour of the expropriation of the landlord is an argument for the transference of the unearned increment of the land to the State. The theoretical basis of nationalisation is to be found in the writings of Ricardo and J. S. Mill. Ricardo defines rent as being "that portion of the produce of the earth which is paid to the landlord for the use of the original and indestructible powers of the soil." If this were so, rent would afford a revenue to the landlord without the landlord rendering any service in the production of wealth. Ricardo was aware that rent in this sense is something different from rent in the popular sense, which includes remuneration to the landlord for capital expended by him upon the land. But the popular writers and orators, such as Henry George, who have caught at his definition, have either forgotten or ignored his qualifying statements[1]. The fundamental principles of land nationalisation are the common property of socialist writers; its philosophical foundation was not laid in this country until the latter part of the eighteenth century. In that period three writers, Thomas Spence, William Ogilvie and Thomas Paine each of them advocated schemes of land reform whereby the iniquity of private property in land, as they regarded it, might be removed. They took their stand on the rights of man to land and life, and they based

---

[1] See *Dictionary of Political Economy*, vol. II, p. 551.

their arguments on that mythical "state of nature" which was so much revered by many of their contemporaries. To quote Spence: "That property in land and liberty among men in a state of nature ought to be equal, few men, one would fain hope, would be foolish enough to deny. Therefore taking this for granted...." Or according to Ogilvie: "Each individual derives from the general right of occupancy a right to an equal share of the soil." Or, again, as Paine has it: "The earth in its uncultivated state was, and ever would have continued to be the common property of the human race."

Though the views of these men and the methods by which they wished to give effect to them varied considerably, each was considered by his contemporaries as a public danger, for any attack on the rights of private property in land was regarded as social heresy, which must be suppressed at all costs. Spence was imprisoned several times for too rash insistence on his views, and the works of both Paine and Ogilvie, the latter in spite of their moderation, were vigorously suppressed as subversive of social order.

To take their schemes individually:

Thomas Spence wished to organise the community on a parochial rather than on a national basis. In a lecture entitled "The Real Rights of Man" given in 1775 he put forward a plan of reform by which the land and all that pertained to it in every parish should be made the property of the parish with powers to make full use of it, but no power to alienate. The holders would pay rent into the parish treasuries which would be expended on the general good. No taxes of any kind would need to be levied as the income provided by these rents would be sufficient to provide for all needs of govern-

ment. In order to attain to this desirable end Spence
wished the nation to cancel the social contract and
reassert its right to the land. He draws an imaginary
picture of how this should be done. "Let all parishioners unite...and enter into a convention, and unani-
mously agree to a Declaration of Rights, in which it is
declared that all the land including coal pits, mines,
rivers, etc. belonging to the Parish of Bees now in the
possession of Lord Drone shall on Lady Day, 25th
March, 18— become Public Property, the Joint Stock
and Common Farm, in which every Parishioner shall
enjoy an equal participation." The property in rents
thus secured by the parish after national and local
government had been provided for was to be divided
equally among all the parishioners. Spence's faith in
his schemes was boundless. To quote his own words,
"Spence's glorious plan is parochial partnership without
private landlords. This just plan will produce ever-
lasting peace and happiness—in fact the Millennium."
A society called "The Spencean Philanthropists,"
formed to carry out his views, did not live very long;
but in the latter part of the nineteenth century "The
English Land Restoration League" expressed views in
many ways very similar to his.

William Ogilvie was a man of very different type. His
outlook was essentially moderate and his projected
reforms are supported by careful reasoning[1]. He declared that the value of land may be divided into three
parts: (1) the value inherent in the soil; (2) the value
created by improvements made by man; (3) the "con-

---

[1] Ogilvie was the author of various works on land tenure:
*A Scheme of Progressive Agrarian Law; Essay on Property; The
Rights of Property in Land.*

tingent value." The landlord is entitled to the improved value of all the land he holds, but should return to the State the rent which accrues from the original and contingent values of the land except that portion of it which he would receive if the land were divided equally among all the citizens, for any land he occupies in excess of this amount should be regarded as a trust held on behalf of the community.

When it came to carrying out his scheme Ogilvie was extremely moderate and fixed his mind on the question of possibility: "Without venturing to make any alterations in landed property regarded with superstitious reverence in this country...many occasions will occur whereof advantage may be taken to introduce under cover of other objects such regulations as may effectually, though indirectly, effect the distribution of property amongst the lowest ranks of the people," and he goes on to explain how individuals and small groups of people can contribute to the desired end.

Thomas Paine embodied his views on land tenure reform in a pamphlet written in 1775–6 entitled *Agrarian Justice opposed to Agrarian Law and to Agrarian Monopoly, being a plan for meliorating the condition of man.* This he would do by creating a National Fund out of which he proposed to pay sums to those arriving at the age of twenty-one to enable them to start life and to those over fifty to help them in their old age. This expensive programme he intended to carry out by a system which should secure for the community the ground rent in land, while leaving the landowner in possession of improvements, etc. due to his own exertions. The best time to secure this ground rent for the nation is at the moment when property is passing by death from one person to another. Paine's programme of reform was far too moderate for Spence by whom it was vigorously attacked.

In the next century Patrick Edward Dove was the first notable writer on the subject, but his views failed to find much popular favour. One of his successors, Henry George, attracted far more notice, though adding nothing new to his doctrine, and many subsequent schemes of land reform drew their original inspiration from his works.

Henry George spent a large part of his life in America, and was greatly impressed by the enormous increase of land values which resulted from the rapid development of that country. He was shocked at the way in which land speculators kept land off the market, and hence out of cultivation, in order to be able to sell it at a big profit so soon as its value had risen sufficiently; and he was also much distressed by the squalid conditions of life in many cities both of England and America. He therefore set out to find a cause and, if possible, a remedy for these conditions and in *Progress and Poverty*, written in 1877, he embodied the results of his investigations. He brought to his self-appointed task considerable literary ability, sublime disregard of facts and a capacity for convincing himself that what he said with sufficient force must be true. Landlords, according to George, could have no claim to their possessions, since though it is obviously just that a man may claim as his right the ownership of that which he himself produces, nevertheless he has no right to claim any proportion of the wealth created by others—and land values originate from this source. The landowner has a certain claim to the improved value of the land, but rent proper should belong to the whole community. As he himself put it: "The truth is, and from this truth there can be no escape, that there is no just title to an exclusive possession of the soil, and that property in land is a bold, bare, enormous wrong, like that of chattel slavery." In fact, all the evils of the time, actual and imaginary, George attributed to the private ownership of land and he stoutly declared that "the wide spreading social evils which everywhere oppress men amid an advancing civilisation spring from a great primary wrong—the appropriation, as the exclusive property of some men, of the land on which and from which all must live. From this fundamental injustice flow all the injustices which condemn the producer of wealth to poverty, and pamper the non-producer in luxury, which rear the tenement house and the palace, plant the brothel behind the church, and compel us to build prisons as we open new schools."

George's plan for the removal of all these evils was simple. He would take from the landlords this rent to which they had no just claim and give it to the community. He was prepared to leave the landlords the value of the improvements they had made in the land, though where these were of long standing, and therefore difficult to estimate, they might be regarded as having been merged in the land value. No other compensation was to be allowed to the landowners. Their claim had no foundation in justice and no compromise can "bridge over the radical difference between right and wrong." George declared that it would be perfectly fair to abolish private "tithes" at one stroke and proclaim the land public property. But this would be difficult to accomplish and he did not propose to effect his reforms by this means. "I do not propose to purchase or confiscate private property in land. The first would be unjust, the second needless. Let the individuals who now hold it still retain, if they want to, possession of what they call their land...we may safely leave them the shell if we take the kernel. It is not necessary to confiscate the land it is only necessary to confiscate rent." This he proposed to do by abolishing all taxation except on land values. He realised that in practice this tax might have to be put on gradually but he hoped that it might finally swallow up all the landlord's ill-gotten gains and leave him only such a small margin as might induce him "to collect the public revenues" by passing on to the State what he received from his tenants. "In this way the State may become the universal landlord without calling herself so, and without assuming a single new function. In form the ownership of land would remain just as it is now. No owner of land need be dispossessed, and no restriction need be placed upon the amount of land any one could hold. For, rent being taken by the State in taxes, land, no matter in whose name it stood, or in what parcels it was held, would be really common property, and every member of the community would participate in the advantages of ownership." This "single tax" system could be easily established, he said, through existing machinery and would save much of the cost of the collection of revenue under the then fiscal system, while the assessment of land values should present no serious difficulty.

Once this reform was established inestimable benefits were to accrue to all classes of society. The system advocated would secure full use of the land, since the holder, being taxed to the full on the land value of his holding and not on the results of his labour, would have every inducement to cultivate to the best of his ability. Moreover, the State would guarantee that security of tenure which is absolutely necessary if the land is to be cultivated to its greatest capacity; for according to Henry George it is the magic of security of tenure, not of ownership, that turns sand into gold.

Henry George's policy was advocated by such societies as the English Land Restoration League, whose aim was "the abolition of landlordism," and whose method has been described as follows: "Don't kick the landlords out, don't buy them out, but TAX them out." This league issued its first manifesto in 1884. It carried on a vigorous campaign in various parts of the country. Later it changed its name to the "English League for the Taxation of Land Values" and declared its aim to be "the restoration of the English land to the English people" by means of the taxation of land values.

The influence of this doctrine was seen later in the opinions of various academic land-reformers their followers, who carried on in Parliament and in the country a strenuous campaign for the placing of all taxation on land values. Their policy was set out clearly by Chomley and Outhwaite[1]. They reaffirmed the doctrine that the landlords could only claim the right to such revenues as sprang from improvements to their land and had no claim to the land value "occasioned by the presence of a population who must have land to live upon." Land values they defined as "the price or rent which could be obtained in an open market

[1] See *The Essential Reform—Land Values Taxation*, Chomley and Outhwaite, 1909.

by land divested of any improvement which may have been made upon it." Both State and Municipality have a right to these land values and the fund thus placed at their disposal should be taxed to the utmost capacity. No other taxes should be imposed till this fund was exhausted.

Arguing from the experience of other countries they suggested that this reform might be effected somewhat as follows: Taxation of land values should not be initiated by a Valuation Bill, which the Lords would veto, but introduced through the Budget. Valuation of land must, of course, precede the collection of the tax, but need not precede its imposition. If the proposals for the imposition, assessment and collection of the tax were included in the Budget the House of Lords could not obstruct the progress of the measure without raising a storm of opposition.

As to the method of assessment. The simplest way to accomplish this would be to require the landowners to send in to the Commissioners of Taxes a return of the unimproved value of their land. If the Commissioners were satisfied with this return they would accept it, or if necessary they would increase it, a right of appeal being left to the tax-payer. Measures would have to be taken to prevent the landlords having to pay income-tax and land-tax on the same property, though as taxation of land values gradually displaced all other taxes this danger would disappear. Various questions such as mortgages, etc. would need special consideration.

According to Chomley and Outhwaite "perfect taxation would abolish private property in land" and this was one of its great assets in their opinion, but they did not propose to interfere with the then landlords, and for so long as they paid the tax on land values they might enjoy absolute ownership. The advantages claimed were substantially the same as those assumed by Henry George. Wages would rise, as the wage earner would have other means of livelihood at hand in the form of land, and moreover as it would be to the advantage of the farmer to cultivate his land to its fullest capacity he would be eager to secure workers. Industry would flourish owing to the improved conditions of the people and the freedom from taxation which it would enjoy. The congestion in town areas would be relieved and the taxation of land values would provide a fund for many social reforms. Moreover, according to these writers, England, in 1909, was "at the parting of the ways where she must choose between land values taxation and the abandonment of Free Trade," of which they declared it to be the logical accompaniment.

Many of the arguments in support of these views were derived from a comparison of the conditions in the colonies and foreign countries, whose case is in no way applicable to England. Moreover, like all single taxers, they grossly exaggerated the revenue which would be provided by such a tax and entirely ignored the fact that landlords have employed the land values, which they were said to have usurped, in improving their lands, thus providing the farmer with capital at little or no interest.

Some years before Henry George wrote his *Progress and Poverty* John Stuart Mill had studied the land problem. In 1870 he became President of the Land Tenure Reform Association. The principal aims of this Association were as follows:

1. To remove all legal and fiscal impediments to the transfer of land.

2. To secure the abolition of the law of primogeniture.

3. To restrict within narrow limits the power of tying up land.

4. To claim for the benefit of the State the future unearned increase of the rent of land, or a great part of that increase which is continuously taking place without effort on the part of the proprietors, merely through the growth of population and wealth.

5. To promote a policy of encouraging co-operative agriculture through the purchase by the State, from time to time, of estates which are in the market, and the letting of them under proper regulations to co-operative associations under the necessary guarantees.

6. To promote the acquisition of land in a similar manner to be let to small cultivators on conditions which, while providing for the proper cultivation of the land, shall secure to the cultivator a durable interest in it.

7. To use Crown lands or lands owned by Public Bodies for the same purpose, and for the improvement of the dwellings of the working classes.

8. To retain for the national use all lands now waste or requiring an Act of Parliament to authorize their inclosure, compensation being made for manorial rights and rights of common.

The members of the Association were very moderate in their views. According to Mill himself their real aim was to remove the remains of feudalism, which had no place in modern society, seeing that the principle that the country belongs to the whole of its inhabitants was firmly established. The land constitutes a natural monopoly and the State, in allowing land to pass into private hands, should have reserved for itself the land value which arises out of this monopoly, since "the land is the original inheritance of all mankind." As shown in item (4) above, in repossessing itself of this right, it is suggested that the State should treat the landowner with liberality and take from him only future increases of value, leaving him in possession of past increases. Moreover, he was to be free to surrender the land to the State at its existing value if this seemed to him preferable to paying the imposed taxation.

In explaining the method by which he thought this reform might be carried out Mill specially stated that it would not be necessary "to enforce the rights of the State to the utmost farthing," and adequate allowance should be made for possible miscalculations. All land should be valued in the first instance and all subsequent improvements registered. Taxation of land values should start as soon as sufficient value had accrued, and care should be taken that such increase was due to general causes and not to improvements performed by the individual. The landlord would further be protected from unjust taxation by the State by being at liberty to relinquish the land at its value as originally ascertained *plus* the value of any later improvements.

Mill declared that this was the extent of the Society's claim with regard to land already in private possession, but as can be seen by the seventh and eighth items of their programme, no fresh land was to become private property.

These views were regarded with disdain by Henry George. He declared that to make a fair and liberal estimate of the market value of the land and then to buy out the owners and merely to take future additions in value for the State would still leave the then owners in possession of vast funds to which they had no claim. Thus, a toll would be constantly levied on labour. Such a plan "is not merely a robbery in the past: it is a robbery in the present—a robbery that deprives of their birthright the infants that are now coming into the world. Why hesitate to make short work of such a system?" He pours scorn on the idea that justice and compensation for landlords can be mentioned in the same breath.

The Land Nationalisation Society was founded in 1881 and its objects were "to affirm that the State holds the land in trust for each generation; to restore to all their natural right to use and enjoy their native land; to obtain for the nation the revenue derived from its labour." Its President was Alfred Russel Wallace.

This Society declared that the fundamental question was the justice or injustice of private property in land, and claimed that "our present land system as a matter of principle is absolutely wrong and perniciously unjust." Landlordism was wrong in principle because, as land is essential to industry and limited in quantity, its possession by individuals creates a monopoly, and such a monopoly is particularly unjust seeing that man cannot exist without access to the land. Moreover "the commercial value of land is the creation of society increasing as population and civilisation increase." Further, private property in land enables the proprietors to appropriate the bulk of the goods produced by the other members of the State and thus keep down wages.

The reformers then went on to state that the following

principles are essential to any satisfactory reform of the present land system:

1. The land, which has been made by no man, and is necessary to human existence, must be made free to all.
2. No man must be allowed to enjoy a greater share of it than another, except by consent of the community and on condition that he pays the community for the privilege which he receives, *i.e.* the economic rent must be returned to the community.
3. Every adult should be enabled to obtain land if he desires so long as he does not interfere with the equal rights of others and pays rent to the State.
4. Occupiers should receive full benefit for any improvements they may make on their land and be allowed full use of it so long as it is not required by the State.

Such reforms, they claimed, were only possible under a system of land nationalisation. This system must provide for the transference of lands to a Trust held on behalf of the community, under the control of the Central Government, but administered locally. Every citizen who wished must be able to obtain land by a simple process; all rent must be paid to the State. This rent must be revised periodically so as to ensure a fair valuation of the land as distinct from the improvement value. All mineral rights should be reserved for the State. A certain measure of compensation should be allowed to the dispossessed landlords, but this should not exceed the net income they obtain from their land.

The Vice-President of the Land Nationalisation Society, writing in 1889, set forth a policy by which a first step in the attainment of these aims might be taken. Local bodies should be popularly elected throughout the country with power to acquire land compulsorily for the State and the lands thus secured should become the absolute property of the State. The landlord should receive compensation in the form of State Bonds. The writer explained that this provision was included because he realised that without it there would be no chance of carrying out his policy. The land once acquired should be let out in limited areas, the tenants being secured of fixity of tenure and of the right to any improvements they might make. They would pay rent direct to the State and have no power to sub-let. All mineral rights should be vested in the community.

Writing in 1914[1] Joseph Hyder, Secretary of the Land Nationalisation Society, expressed views very similar to those advocated by the Society in 1881. He stated that owing to the small use which local authorities had made of their powers to acquire land for various purposes, it was clear that no complete system of land nationalisation was possible unless carried out by the central authority from whom in the last resort all such powers must be derived, although the Municipal authorities might play an important part. He suggested that as an initial step the State might create a "National Commission or Land Board," which would buy up estates as they came on the market, and in this way a considerable amount of land might be acquired by the State.

A fair valuation could be secured by the introduction of a "tax-and-buy" principle, *i.e.* "the national valua-

[1] See *The Case for Land Nationalisation*, Joseph Hyder, 1914.

tion must be the basis of either taxing land or buying it, at the discretion of the public authorities." This should ensure a fair valuation being placed on the land, for the owners would not wish to be too highly valued as they would be rated on that valuation; whereas if the valuation were too low the State would be able to acquire land on easy terms.

The purchase of the land by the nation could be financed, he suggested, by the issue of "Compensation Bonds" on which the State could pay the interest in most cases out of the rents which it would receive. These bonds should terminate after a sufficient period of time to secure the just rights of the landowners, say in seventy-five or eighty years, but the State should retain the option of redeeming them at any time prior to their termination at their current market value. A part of the unearned increment might be devoted to that purpose. In most cases these Compensation Bonds "would represent the simple capitalisation of present *net* rent." But in the case of land near towns, etc., prospective values would have to be allowed for in the purchase price, as the owner might have withdrawn money from productive investments in order to secure such lands. This money would, of course, have to be raised from some other source, but as the prospective values were gradually realised they could be applied to paying off the loans made to cover the initial deficit. Under such a system it is true that the State would be creating a huge debt, but it would be securing at the same time huge assets, and the advantages which land nationalisation would bring would soon counterbalance any temporary disadvantages.

Thus, the Land Nationalisation Society was opposed

to the principle of the taxation of land values. Joseph Hyder said if all that its advocates claimed for it were true the system of securing the eventual possession of the land for the State by the taxation of land values would be a serious rival to the system of land national-isation by purchase. But on consideration he found that such a system was neither practicable, just nor effective. It would be very difficult to bring into operation, and since the sub-letting of lands would not be interfered with the tax might be handed on to the tenants. As to justice, Hyder declared that it was unfair to take lands from their then owners by taxation rather than by compensation, because "private property in land is a mistake, not a crime." The Government and nation had for generations given their sanction to the institu-tion of private property in land and those then in enjoyment of it had acquired it with the connivance of the whole nation. Moreover, such a system would hit the poor as well as the rich landowner, and leave un-touched those who had invested their money in other commodities. Under such circumstances it was clear that a system which combined land nationalisation with compensation for landlords was fairer than "a policy of taxing the landlords out of existence."

None of these schemes have made an appeal to any considerable section of the community, and to-day they are only of historical interest. Starting, for the most part, from the premiss that private property in land is immoral, most of the proposals for its transfer to the State are frankly confiscatory in their intent. There is no body of support for this view; it may be expedient to supersede the landowner, as it is the object of the present study to suggest, but public opinion is not prepared to condemn him, nor to acquiesce in offering him anything less than a square deal in those cases in which his supersession is considered necessary.

The provisions of Mr Lloyd George's well-remembered Budget, embodied in the Finance Act (1909–10), 1910, were inspired, no doubt, by the arguments of the Single-Tax group, but in effect they recognised not only the right to private property in land but also the landlord's right to "unearned increment." All that the Act provided was that the State should participate with the private owner in the increment value created by the community. Taxes were to be levied on leasehold reversions; on land awaiting development; on mining royalties; nowhere was it suggested that confiscation or even State purchase should be attempted. The short-lived Agriculture Act, 1920, passed by Mr Lloyd George's Coalition Government carried matters a stage further in the direction of State control in that it provided for the administration, under the State, of the landlord's estate in those cases in which it was found that the standard of management fell below a certain level. The Ministry of Agriculture was empowered to assume control and to administer the property in the interests of production from the soil, regardless of the landlord's wishes or finances[1]. This measure was never tested in working as it was repealed within a few months of its enactment. Liberal political thought, however, continued to develop and from its proposals for the improvement of rural industry as set out at the recent election it is clear that its policy to-day is not far removed from the land nationalisation programme of the Labour Party. The philosophical grounds for State

[1] See p. 3, *ante*.

ownership have largely disappeared; the landlord is to be displaced because he is regarded as a stumbling-block in the path of progress, or because, in some ill-defined way, the country is suffering from "the vestiges of feudalism." These parties do not seem to consider that modern economic conditions are making it increasingly difficult, and, in many cases, impossible for him to carry out his part in the agricultural partnership; they suggest rather that he has no part in it to play. It will have been gathered that it is from motives diametrically opposed to these that the consideration of the acquisition of the land by the State is advocated here. The landlord free to function is, it is urged, an element in rural society essential to its best interests, and it is only because of events which tend more and more to restrict his scope for action that his supersession is suggested.

II. PRESENT PROPOSALS

A study of the proposals for the nationalisation of the land briefly outlined in the foregoing pages will make it plain that the outstanding practical difficulty, if schemes merely confiscatory in their intent are ruled out, is the formulation of workable proposals for land purchase. Those of the Land Nationalisation Society based on acquisition at current market value (see p. 38) came nearest to that which might be termed practical, as they contemplated the simple capitalisation of the net rent. If they had stopped here they might form a basis upon which to work, but they included some allowance for "prospective values," and whilst this is obviously equitable, where the intention is other than spoliation, it is quite unworkable as a practical scheme. Prospective values are so much matters of opinion, and so little questions of fact, that in any attempt to assess them provision would be needed for appeals by claimants from any valuations made by the State. Thus, the work of valuation would be no sooner begun than it would be blocked completely by innumerable appeals to arbitration on the question of the amount of compensation payable for deferred and potential values; and the whole machinery would break down.

Probably the most extensive and certainly the most general of these prospective values is that claimed for land which may be required for building development, and the difficulty of framing a scheme for the expropriation of the landlord at once equitable and workable would be enormously reduced if land falling within this category could be eliminated. Building-land, and land with prospective building value are met with, almost exclusively, in and around town areas, and the proposal under the scheme about to be outlined is that State acquisition should be confined to agricultural lands and other forms of property falling *outside* all urban administrative areas. Thus all lands, whether agricultural or not, included within any of the following units of local government would be exempted from the operation of this land purchase scheme:

Counties of Cities.
Counties of Towns.
County Boroughs.
Municipal Boroughs.
Urban Districts.
Land falling within the area of a Town Planning Scheme approved by the Ministry of Health under secs. 42–48 of the Housing, Town Planning, etc., Act, 1919.

It will be realised that the problem of the ownership of building-land, whether actual or potential, is a thing apart from the present consideration, the only object of which is the recognition of the fact of the passing of the rural landowner and the provision of the least inefficient substitute for him. Some agricultural land is to be met within the limits of the areas defined above, but the quantity is relatively negligible and it may be disregarded. Outside such areas the proposal is that all lands, speaking generally, should be acquired by the State. It may be desirable to make exceptions in particular cases; for example, property already in the ownership of certain public administrative authorities, such as asylums and industrial schools, and the farm-lands frequently attached to them; reservoirs, water-works and sewage farms; commons; railways and canals; churchyards and burial grounds; rectory and vicarage houses and gardens. These and any similar properties might be excluded; but no exception is contemplated in the case of any holdings which are the property of County Councils, nor of Crown, Charity or Church lands.

The valuation of the property to be taken over would be a mere matter of arithmetic in the great majority of cases. The State is provided already with the calculation of the annual value of every holding in the country, which is made for income-tax purposes. This valuation is based on the rent received by the landlord in the case of properties let, and on the rent estimated in the case of the owner-occupier; deductions from the rent are made for all fixed out-goings and for maintenance, and thus the net annual value is arrived at. This valuation is kept up-to-date by periodical revision, so that in the simple case, and with the exclusion of the urban areas nearly every case would fall in this class, the purchase price would be got by the capitalisation of the income-tax assessments. Mr Lloyd George's land valuation broke down because it sought to ascertain original and theoretical values which have long been obscured—if, indeed, they ever had any existence—in a country where the soil has been wrought upon and developed to the extent that it has in England; and the mass of the people concerned were not prepared to enter into the speculations involved. On the other hand, the land valuation for income assessment is based on the outstanding fact of ownership—the rent received by the landlord—and it is understood and accepted by all classes; moreover, it exists. The only question for consideration, therefore, is the number of years' purchase at which the income-tax assessment should be capitalised, and this would depend upon the value of money at the time of the transaction; at the present moment twenty-two and a half years' purchase of the Schedule A assessment would represent, presumably, something about the purchase price. Thus, in the case where the Schedule A assessment of a farm-house, buildings and land is £297, the purchase consideration would be £297 × 22½, or £6682. 10s.

Special cases would at once arise in which valuation by this simple calculation would be inequitable. Woodlands are a case in point. They are valued for income-tax assessment at the unimproved, or prairie value of the land, so that the landlord would receive nothing for his crop of timber. This difficulty could be met by adding to the capitalised valuation figure for the land a sum representing the present value of the estimated worth of the timber at maturity. Thus, if the assess-

ment, at prairie value, of a woodland of 48 acres is
£17. 16s., and the value of the timber at maturity in
10 years time was estimated at £120 per acre, or
£5760 in all, the calculation of the sum payable to the
owner would be as follows:

	£	s.	d.
Land:			
£17. 16s. × 22½	400	10	0
Timber:			
£5760 deferred 10 years	3709	0	6
Total	£4109	10	6

This method of valuing growing timber as a crop has
long been in practice in some localities in connection
with underwoods, and no new principle is involved. In
the case of young plantations not exceeding, say, twenty
years' growth, an assessment of maturity value would
be, probably, too speculative, and the cost of trees and
planting, together with compound interest at 4½ per
cent., might be substituted as the figure to be added to
the prairie value of the land to arrive at the total sum
due to the landlord.

Leaseholds would furnish another example of the
cases calling for special provision. Here there are two
values, the ground rent and the structure upon it, and
two persons to be bought out, the ground landlord and
the lessee. The valuation both of the ground rent and
of the buildings is a simple calculation as before, and
the only question to be considered is the apportionment
of the consideration to be paid for the buildings between
the lessee and the reversioner. Here again, a simple
solution seems possible by assigning to the ground
landlord the present value of his reversion, and to the
leaseholder the remainder. Taking the case of a building

lease at a ground rent of £10 with 40 years to run, with premises erected on the land valued together for income-tax at £120:

$$£$$

Land:
£10 × 22½ = 225
Buildings:
£110 × 22½ = 2475
Total £2700

	£	s.	d.
Now the Present Value of £2475 deferred 40 years	= 425	10	6
Thus: Ground landlord's interest is			
£225 + £425. 10s. 6d. =	650	10	6
And Lessee's interest is £2475 − £425. 10s. 6d. =	2049	9	6
	£2700	0	0

It may be supposed that the leasehold system will not survive much longer in its present form. The objections to it are common property of all but the most reactionary, and an equitable measure for leasehold enfranchisement would meet with little opposition. For the purposes of the present consideration, too, it should be noted that by the exclusion of urban areas from the operation of State purchase very few leaseholds would be encountered.

Another special case is that of the owner-occupiers, whether of mansions, parks and sporting rights, of farms, of houses and gardens, or of shops and other premises. These persons enjoy, at present, complete fixity of tenure, and provision would be necessary to secure to them an equal status under the State acquisition scheme. This could be done by giving them an option on a tenancy, for a term not exceeding their own lives, or for the lives of their wives or of the survivors of them, or for a period of ten years—whichever should be the longest—with liberty to surrender the tenancy at the end, say, of the third year from sale or of any multiple of this period, but without power to sub-let. An alternative to this arrangement, which might receive consideration, would be to defer the conveyance of property occupied by the owner until his occupancy ceased by death or by voluntary surrender; but on various grounds it would probably be held undesirable to make an exception of these cases from the general provisions as to purchase by the State.

Other special cases may have to be considered, but there is no reason to anticipate difficulty in providing for them. There remains one important case, however, which must be met, namely that of land for which the owner claims a value beyond that accruing from its immediate use; for example, prospective building value, and mineral rights. The exclusion of land within urban areas from State purchase, would reduce very materially the claims for prospective building values, but some would certainly be made, and claims for minerals and other future increments might be numerous. In all such cases no attempt should be made to assess the additional value claimed; the task is virtually impossible and to embark upon it would be to bring the whole machinery to a standstill. The value according to the present use of the land should be ascertained by the means proposed, but its acquisition by the State at the figure arrived at should be deferred for, say, ten years[1]. During this period the owner should be free to develop it for the purpose for which he thinks it is of value. The whole or any part developed thus would be

---

[1] The deferred period might be more or less than ten years; this is obviously a matter for discussion.

conveyed at the revised Sch. A valuation (unless the form taken by development should bring it under the category of exceptions) at the expiration of ten years; the whole or any part not developed during this period would pass to the State at the original valuation. Lands supposed to possess a prospective building value, or to contain minerals, are examples of cases which would be covered by these provisions. In the case of alleged building-land, the erection of houses or buildings within the period of grace should be the only evidence acceptable in support of the owner's claim for consideration under this head. This would anticipate cases which might otherwise occur in which an owner attempted to defeat the objects of the scheme by a bogus sale of undeveloped land at a high figure to a Land Company, all the shares in which were held by himself. In the case of minerals, hardship might arise if recognition were only to be accorded to mineral rights which were developed during the period of grace. Coal, for example, may be known to exist under an estate, but under the normal development of mining in the locality it might not be reached within the time-limit proposed. In these circumstances any *bona fide* sale of mining rights should be recognised, and the acquisition of property by the State should be limited to the surface rights.

For there is no intention, under this scheme for State purchase, to attempt to nationalise industry; as has been stated before, the proposals put up for consideration here have their origin solely in the breakdown of the landlord system, not in its iniquity, and nothing is further from their purpose than interference with private enterprise. Thus it is that the omission from State purchase of mines and quarries in operation, or of mining rights sold *bona fide*, is proposed. These enterprises together with surface rights necessary to their working and development would remain in private ownership.

Private persons desirous of building on land which has become State property under this scheme would acquire leases from the State. On the death of themselves, or of their wives, or of the survivors of them, or after ten years—whichever should be the longest—the State would acquire the lessee's interest upon the basis of the Schedule A income-tax assessment multiplied by the years' purchase applicable at the time of the transaction. Provision could be made, if necessary, for surrender by the lessee after due notice. Slightly different conditions would be needed in the case of persons or corporations desirous of erecting factories or other buildings for industrial purposes, but they present no special difficulty.

This is, then, the scheme designed to give effect to this proposal for the supersession by the State of the private owner of land. Briefly, it contemplates the purchase of extra-urban property at the capitalised value of the property-tax assessment with an option to the vendor to defer conveyance for a certain period of years in cases where potential values are claimed.

As regards the conveyance of the property acquired, nothing beyond a possessory title would be required of the vendors. All the work preliminary to conveyance, and the conveyance itself, would be done by the State without expense to the vendor, except in so far as he might wish to employ professional assistance. The nucleus of the organisation needed for this work already exists in the Land Valuation Department.

Coming, now, to the question of how to finance land-purchase by the State, the transaction would be necessarily a paper one. There could be no option to the vendor to take payment for his property in cash, but *National Land Stock* would be issued to him to the value of the property passing. This stock should bear interest at a rate comparable with the yield of other long-dated British Government stocks at the time of its issue, and a bond issue on equal terms would probably be useful and popular with a certain section of the vendor public. Both stock and bonds should be redeemable at a long date through the creation of a sinking-fund, and if its operation were postponed, say, until ten years after the inception of the scheme, it is likely that the surplus revenue accruing to the State after payment of the expenses of administration and the debt service would be sufficient for sinking-fund purposes without imposing any charge upon the exchequer.

It may be asked how this can be, seeing that the whole case for buying-out the present owners of the land is based on the fact that they can no longer finance the equipment of their estates as a business proposition. The question is partly answered by the scheme of administration described in the next Chapter, under which considerable economies in management may be expected, but more fully by the probability that, taking a long view, the land *as a whole* is a profitable investment. Even to-day properties can be cited which give a commercial return to their owners, the medium and inferior lands being set off by more fertile tracts and by portions in the process of active development; the trouble is that the profitable and the unprofitable are sharply segregated in the majority of cases, and the owners of unremunerative swings have no money-spinning roundabouts to adjust their financial balances.

The magnitude of the transaction involved can only roughly be estimated; the reports of the Commissioners of Inland Revenue do not admit of the exact computation of the amount of the income derived from the ownership of lands[1]. The last figures quoted in the *Statistical Abstract* from their Reports are those for the financial year 1921–22[2], when the gross income derived from the occupation of lands in England and Wales returned under Schedule A of the income-tax was £36,660,000, but it must be remembered that there has been a new valuation for property-tax carried out since the War, which came into force in 1923–24, and these figures no longer represent current values. Assuming that rents, generally, have risen by about 20 per cent. since the last pre-war valuation, and allowing for the purchase of property other than agricultural land, such as timber, and houses, the total annual value to be capitalised for purchase might approximate to £50,000,000. On the basis of 22½ years' purchase this is equivalent to a capital sum of £1,125,000,000. These figures, however,

[1] The following Parliamentary question and answer are of interest:

Major Wheler asked the Chancellor of the Exchequer the amount of property-tax collected from land under Schedules A and B during the year 1921–2.

Mr Snowden: I regret that this information is not available as, under the present system of graduation and differentiation of the income-tax, with personal allowances, deductions and reliefs appurtenant, not to the various sources of income charged under each Schedule, but to the total income of the tax-payer, the total yield cannot be divided between the respective Schedules.

(*Hansard*, 15th July, 1924; Question No. 51.)

[2] Cmd. 2207, p. 39.

must be taken as being little more than guesses, but they serve to show that the financial side of the problem is not one which should present any difficulty.

Opposition to a financial transaction of this nature and magnitude may be expected from the Treasury and from what may be called the banker interest. It will be objected that the creation of a great new issue of National Land Stock will impair national credit and add to the cost of government borrowing; that the country has with difficulty succeeded in restoring the gold standard and that it is being asked at once to embark upon a scheme which can only result in fresh "inflation." Even though this should be its effect it could only be temporary; but the probability is that it would never be perceptible because there would be no possibility of anything approaching a sudden issue of a thousand millions or so of stock. The processes of valuation and transfer of estates could not be carried through in a week or two, and the Land Stock would, in fact, be issued very gradually over a considerable term of years. England has multiplied her national debt, through the War, to an immensely greater amount and yet has returned to the gold standard, so that the relatively small transaction contemplated here should cause no real embarrassment.

CHAPTER IV

STATE ADMINISTRATION

THE administration of the lands after their acquisition by the State is a problem calling for serious consideration. Anything in the nature of "management from Whitehall" would be fatal to efficiency in the control of the very large area involved. It is essential that the power to make decisions on points of every-day administration should be decentralised; what is needed is a system resembling as closely as possible that which exists under private ownership to-day, where responsibility is vested in the hands of agents answerable for their actions to their principals. Like agriculture itself, land-agency is a business the conduct of which calls for prompt decisions by the man-on-the-spot, and any system of control based on reference in every case to a superior authority in London would break down completely in practice. For this reason it is not contemplated that the creation of a new Ministry to deal with a business so great even as that of administration of the estates of rural England would be necessary. The work would devolve upon a new branch of the Ministry of Agriculture and Fisheries, the *Administration of Lands Branch*, under the direction of a *Chief Administrator of Lands*. This office would be largely an accounting institution; it would be the channel of communication between the local administrators and the Board of Inland Revenue; it would prepare estimates of revenue; it would be responsible for the transmission of Cabinet policy towards land and its development to the local administrators and for the execution of this policy by them. It would be concerned with the staffing of the local administrative offices and all questions of personnel, recruitment and promotion in the administrative service. It should be laid down in the clearest possible language that no question of ordinary estate management should be the concern of the central administration, but, on the contrary, that such work should devolve exclusively upon the local organisation.

The local administration would be organised, in the first place, upon a county basis; the County is so generally adopted, nowadays, as the unit of organisation for so many purposes that its selection for that now under consideration is almost inevitable. No doubt certain adjustments might be necessary in the direction of splitting some of the large ones, or uniting others, or parts of them, but this need not be considered here. Each administrative county area would be under the control of a *County Land Agent*, responsible to the Chief Administrator of Lands, and the County would be sub-divided into administrative districts each of them under the charge of a *District Land Agent* responsible to the County Land Agent. The extent of the Districts would vary with the intensity of the agriculture within them, but if the normal District were to contain, approximately, some 30,000 acres it would be no larger than the average well-qualified agent could supervise.

Clerical staffs for the County and for the District Land Agents would complete the local organisation.

The work of the District Agents would resemble in all particulars that of the agent on any large private estate. The letting of farms; the supervision of the tenants; the execution of repairs to houses and buildings; questions of land drainage, cottage building and other forms of estate development; the collection of rents; in fact, all the usual routine of administration would devolve upon the District Land Agent, and in any matter of doubt or difficulty he would refer to the County Land Agent very much as the private agent now refers to his principal. The tenants, too, should be able to refer a decision by the District Agent to the County Agent, so as to put them in a position equal to that which many of them now enjoy, when they can have access to the landlord himself.

The clerical staffs of the District Land Agents would, of course, include draughtsmen and clerks-of-works, able to prepare plans and specifications under the direction of the agent, and to supervise their execution by contractors.

The Land Agents, both County and District, would be recruited, in the first instance, from the body of those already engaged in the administration of property. As regards the District Agents, a system of graded salaries could be adopted with advantage; not only would this be desirable by reason of the variations in the degree of responsibility devolving upon agents in respect of their several districts, but also it would allow of promotion during the period of service. Within the grades promotion would be by seniority, but promotion from one grade to the next should proceed by ability. Subsequently, admission to the administration branch of the service would be by examination. University agricultural departments and agricultural colleges would be natural training grounds for these entrance examinations, and the students successful in them would be gazetted to the county offices as vacancies arose in the lowest division, which would be a non-graded class known as that of *Temporary Assistant*. After a specified period of service the Temporary Assistants would be allowed to present themselves for a further examination qualifying them for the lowest grade of the District Agent class. Temporary Assistants unsuccessful in passing into this grade within a specified period of time would automatically leave the service.

The organisation of the clerical staff would proceed upon similar lines. It, too, would be a graded service, and admission to it, in the first instance, would be by a literary examination, followed at a later date by a more technical test in subjects of estate office routine as the qualification for permanent establishment in the service.

It is claimed that an administrative organisation of this kind would attract into the service men of the highest ability. The work itself is of a nature to make a strong appeal to young men, and the fact that entry into the service, and promotion within it, would depend upon ability and not upon influence, coupled with the prospect of steady employment leading up to a pension upon retirement, would attract to the administration of property men of education, capacity and enterprise to a degree by no means universal to-day.

It has been stated above that the local organisation would consist of the professional and clerical staffs. This takes no account of the considerable staffs of workmen of all kinds maintained on many estates; for it is not contemplated by this system that estate works would be carried out by direct labour. In theory, the maintenance of the estate by means of a staff of estate employees ensures good work and saves the contractor's profits; in practice, it is difficult to secure that degree of efficiency in control by estate foremen which the contractor's self-interest guarantees. "Who subscribed half-a-million to the War Loan?" asked an estate joiner taken to task for wasting his employer's time on a millionaire-owner's estate, and this is too frequently the attitude of the estate employee towards his duty to his employer. Moreover, on a large property much time is lost by a staff, necessarily centralised, in getting to and from work on the out-lying parts of the estate. On the other hand, the allocation of estate repairs, new buildings, fencing, draining, etc. amongst local firms and workmen would do much to maintain the distribution throughout the countryside of the village tradesmen and craftsmen, whose disappearance is the subject of general comment.

No particular reference has been made so far to the question of Forestry. The acquisition of land by the State would bring under control a very large area of woodland extending, in England, to something like 1,700,000 acres. For the first time it would be possible to secure economic forest management in this country, and the problem of management is a very serious one. Three courses appear to be possible. The first is to make each District Land Agent responsible for the economic development of the woodlands within his District just as the agent on the privately-owned estate is to-day. This course would introduce the smallest element of change into the present system of estate management; but there would be little else to say in its favour. If forestry is to have a chance it will require the application of more technical knowledge than the

District Agent will possess; moreover, the distribution of woodlands is so unequal as to make it undesirable to train the agents up to the requisite pitch. Again, in the majority of cases, the District would not contain woodlands to an extent sufficient to make an economic working unit, and it is clear that control must be organised on a larger basis.

The second course that suggests itself is to create a class of administrators to be known as *County Foresters*, qualified men, trained at one of the recognised forestry institutions. Each County Land Agent would be provided with one or more of these officers on his staff who would be responsible to him for the administration of the woodlands of the County. The proportion of woodland varies considerably in different Counties, and this would admit of a system of grading and promotion in the forestry branch of the service which would be all to the good; at the same time, it is probable that even the least wooded County would furnish a timber area large enough to engage a full time forester and to make an economic unit for development and exploitation, whilst most would require several.

The other advantages of this course are that it would admit of a very close *liaison* between the managers of woodland and of agricultural land, both being united under the same administrative chief in the person of the County Agent. This is of considerable importance, for the land agents would be big users of local timber of all kinds, and questions of estate management affecting them and the foresters alike would arise, not infrequently, in every-day working.

The County Foresters would require staffs of working

woodmen for the ordinary routine of planting, felling, nursery work, and so on. These would be recruited in the labour market in the ordinary way, and would not form part of the established service.

The third course would be to take all the acquired woodlands out of the control of the Administration of Lands Service, and to hand them over to the Forestry Commission. This course would probably commend itself to some, but there are serious objections to it. The Forestry Commission is rather of the nature of an historical accident, the result of the breakdown of other administrative expedients. There are no parallels for its creation or existence, and it suffers from serious disabilities in working. Moreover, its perpetuation under the land-purchase scheme proposed would introduce an undesirable element of dual control into the administration of the countryside, and it would be impossible to secure that degree of co-ordination of the work of the agricultural and forest services which would be essential to effective development. Such questions as the withdrawal of land from agriculture for afforestation in this locality or that would be bound to arise, and the difficulty of determining policy would be greatly enhanced if two authorities, independent of each other, were concerned.

The balance of advantage seems, therefore, to lie in the second course, namely that which contemplates the provision of a service of County Foresters attached to the staffs of the County Land Agents. If this were adopted, the Forestry Commission would, presumably, cease to function unless as a body to advise the Treasury upon applications for grants in aid of education and research.

The administrative scheme briefly outlined here is capable of considerable development in detail. Although it is contemplated that all land in rural areas should be vested in the State, and while the State should always reserve powers to intervene if things should go wrong, there is much to be said for delegating powers to representative bodies whenever it is likely that there will be reasonably efficient control. It has been suggested already that certain exceptions must also be made (see p. 44), and water-works form a good example; many large towns draw their water and own large catchment areas at long distances from their own borders, as, for example, at Vyrnwy and Rhayader, in Wales, which serve Liverpool and Birmingham respectively. In these, and in kindred cases, the present state of affairs would have to be left essentially undisturbed. Again, a case could be made out for the creation, outside of the scheme, of a Department of State Lands which would administer lands serving obviously national purposes. These might include mountains, open spaces, military lands (such as Salisbury Plain), foreshores, etc.; such lands have little direct economic purpose. As regards delegation of State administrative powers, there is no reason why a body such as the National Trust should be superseded wherever it has the management of property, so long as it performs a useful function, and the numerous *ad hoc* bodies which administer large commons might be allowed to continue.

At this stage, however, the problem is the administration of land in the mass, and the consideration in detail of exemptions from State control and of the delegation of State authority in particular cases, is one which can be undertaken, if necessary, at a later stage.

CHAPTER V

GAINS AND LOSSES

L ET it be stated, over again, that no advantage, on balance, is claimed for this system of land-purchase when contrasted with the system of private ownership which has prevailed so long; it is only put forward to provide an orderly way out of the difficulties which the breakdown of the old system is creating. But though the disappearance of the landowner is regarded as an irreparable loss to the rural community, it is satisfactory to be able to forecast certain definite advantages which might be expected to accrue from State purchase of the land.

The State itself would gain in several directions. Reference has been made already to the need for State-aid to agriculture, which might conceivably arise, and to the difficulty of providing it under a system of private ownership of land[1]. But though this contingency may be rather remote in the cases already enumerated it is by no means unlikely to arise, and there are other situations of immediate import in which the State is concerned where the difficulty of action under the present conditions of tenure asserts itself. The provision of cheap capital for example, for much needed estate improvements, e.g. farm buildings, farm cottages, land drainage, etc. is urgent, and might be undertaken by public assistance in the interests of agricultural production, but what steps could be taken by the State to secure a fair repayment in those cases where the improvement was successful?

[1] See p. 8.

Again, there is the vital question of the maintenance of arable farming and the proper use of the land—how are these to be secured? Although the statements which appear, from time to time, as to the degree of under-farming in England are often much exaggerated it is common knowledge that there is too much of it, and it is the cry of all the political parties that the situation must be dealt with. The proposals of the Liberal Land Committee for an extension of occupying-ownership will do nothing to meet the case—in fact, they may very well aggravate it, for the owner-occupier is responsible only to himself. Nor has the Labour Party's scheme for giving further powers to the County Agricultural Committees to enforce cultivation any merit; "orders" to farm are quite unworkable. The only person who can apply the necessary pressure is the landlord, and the only basis for the proper direction of farming is the contract of tenancy. If the State were constituted universal landlord it would be possible to define the conditions subject to which the land was to be held so as to maintain the maximum possible amount of cultivation. In this way only can the community secure the fullest use of the land, namely by laying down the conditions of tenure and leaving the farmer free to develop his enterprise subject to them. This is not socialism; it is, in fact, the antithesis to the socialism that aims at controlling the farmer's business methods.

Other advantages of this scheme for the public acquisition of agricultural land are summarised below:

A. To the State

(1) The provision of land for all public purposes, such as building, railway construction, road-making and other works of improvement would be a simple matter

of routine so soon as determined upon in the public interest. Protracted negotiations, expensive arbitration cases, slow and cumbersome conveyancing, all these things would be obviated, and it must be admitted that they can constitute a serious abuse.

(2) Land Settlement. There is not much reason to suppose that the demand for Small Holdings will ever become extensive in England. The life is too laborious and the returns from it too small to be attractive to men in a country so highly industrial, where hours of labour and rates of wages become daily more and more the matters of control and regulation, and where only the few are likely to take their chance as the masters of their own destinies. Such men are to be encouraged, however, as men of industry and character, and as the smaller units of cultivation tend to yield more in gross product and to give more employment than the larger ones, it is in the interest of the State to provide them as required. On the whole the experience of the County Councils seems to be that land could be hired or bought in most cases without difficulty, but whatever trouble may arise sometimes would go, and the expenses of acquisition, valuation and conveyancing, would be saved, if the State were landlord.

(3) Afforestation and the development of the timber resources of the country would be stimulated. Few private estates are large enough to justify the employment of a qualified forester, and economic forestry may be said hardly to exist anywhere in the country. Afforestation of new areas is a financial impossibility to the private landlord, and the operations of the Forestry Commission, or of some agency substituted for it, would be greatly facilitated by the proposals here put forward.

Nothing could be more inimical to forestry than that which happens on the break-up of private estates. Nobody wants the woodlands; if they contain marketable timber they are bought and laid waste by enterprising timber-merchants; otherwise they are included with other lots and the buyer leaves them to take care of themselves until such time as something can be made of them by their destruction. The State never dies, and becoming possessed of all the woodlands of the country it could secure qualified management and it would introduce that degree of continuity of policy which, though vital to conservation and development, is impossible so long as the life of the owner is so much less than the life of the tree.

(4) The heavy burden on land imposed by the present cumbersome and costly system of conveyancing would be lifted. Outside the County of London no facilities for the registration of title are provided, and even under the Law of Property Act, 1922, it will not be possible to introduce the system before 1936, and then only by very slow stages. To sell land to the value of £100 may cost the vendor to-day twenty times as much as the transfer of an equivalent amount of War Loan.

(5) The administrative machinery required for the assessment and collection of certain taxes and charges on property would be greatly reduced. Income-tax falling under Schedule A—the property-tax—would go, and the money collected under this head at very great expense would be secured to the State by the process, at once simpler and cheaper, of deduction at the source[1].

[1] The cost of assessment and collection of property-tax cannot be separated from that of other taxes, but it is necessarily heavy in proportion to the amount yielded when contrasted with other schedules.

Another saving in the cost of administration would be the expense of dealing with the claims of landlords for repayment of income-tax on that part of their income expended on the maintenance of their estates in excess of the statutory allowances for this purpose. Since this concession was first made under Mr Lloyd George's Finance Act (1909–10) of 1910, the rise in the rate of taxation has made it one of great importance to the landlord, and there must be comparatively few estates which do not involve the Inland Revenue Authority in the scrutiny of claims under this head.

(6) Similarly, land-tax would disappear, and the cost of assessment, collection and, here and there, of redemption would go. What this amounts to cannot be stated, as it is inseparably bound up with that of other Inland Revenue duties, but probably it is relatively small.

Another small saving would be effected by the extinction of copyholds, and the Government could take in hand the whole question of tithe redemption, which would effect a considerable saving in the administrative machinery when completed.

(7) A great saving in the cost of estate administration might be expected, and, at the same time, an increase of efficiency arising out of the consolidation of the administrative unit. There are many estates too small to give full-time employment to their administrators; there are many more where the loss of efficiency involved in the management of their scattered members is very heavy. Ecclesiastical and charity lands scattered all over the country afford bad examples; but private estates are, many of them, equally badly assembled as regards efficiency of management. A case may be cited,

by no means extreme, of a property of about 21,000
acres; it consisted of one block of about 7000 acres
practically ring-fenced; eight miles to the north was an
outlier of about 3000 acres, another of about 700 acres
six miles to the north-west, a third of about 600 acres
some nine miles to the west, a fourth of about 2000
acres six miles to the south-west, a fifth of about 600
acres ten miles to the south-east; whilst forty miles to
the south lay another large block of about 7000 acres.
Not only is the cost of administration increased by
such a unit, but its efficiency is seriously diminished.
Adequate supervision of farming is impossible and the
control of estate workmen, foresters and contractors is
of necessity loose. Under State ownership the land
would be blocked out into areas differing in size
according to the intensity of the agricultural industry
within them, but each of them delimited so as to provide
maximum employment at minimum effort to their
administrators.

(8) The preservation of places of historical interest
and natural beauty would be facilitated. The lack of
means to repair and sustain, or the need of money to be
made from exploitation, has led to the destruction of
many beautiful buildings and the loss of many beauty
spots. Moreover, it would be possible to preserve and
examine the contents of estate offices and muniment
rooms. What is happening to estate maps, rentals and
all the accumulated records, some of great historical
interest, on the break-up of the old estates? It is to be
feared that not infrequently they fall into the hands of
those who cannot assess their value, whereas many of
them should be stored in national collections and made
available for the student and research-worker.

As to losses, almost the only way in which the State could suffer would be in the yield of the Stamp Duty. The proportion paid on the transfer of property in rural areas cannot, of course, be stated; on land and houses in general the yield during the past four years has been[1]:

			£
1920–1	...	...	5,147,242
1921–2	...	...	3,118,615
1922–3	...	...	2,940,825
1923–4	...	...	4,151,234

However much of this may be estimated to represent duties on the conveyance of agricultural land and rural houses, the amount must be relatively trivial.

An objection may be advanced by those who fear that the organised tenants could use so much political influence that the State would never receive a fair rent for its land. The danger does not seem very real. The private landlord to-day can hardly be said, in many cases, to receive a fair rent, partly owing to his patriarchical relations with his tenants, partly to the retail nature of his business, and partly because anything that can be regarded at all as a good holding cannot be said ever to come into the open market. Thus, although there is a demand for farms that is not yet satisfied it is not effective in raising rents to the economic limit. In these circumstances it is difficult to understand how the State could find itself at a disadvantage, in contrast to the private landlord, in coming to fair terms with its tenants.

---

[1] These figures are eloquent of the activity in the land market following the end of the war, and of the subsequent slump.

B. To the Landlord

Since the whole of this scheme for State purchase rests on the increasing difficulty of the landlord in continuing to function, the ways in which he would gain can be left to inference. Two examples may be quoted, however, of the financial advantages accruing to the landlord when liberated from the burden of estate maintenance; they furnish striking illustrations of the inducement to the landlord to give up the struggle, though it is not to be inferred that landlords generally would obtain results commensurate with them under the scheme for State Purchase.

The first is taken from the report of a well-known hospital:

The area sold has totalled about 10,000 acres, and at a low estimate the hospital has gained thereby additional income of £10,000 a year, after deducting expenses.

One of the reasons which made our Governors hesitate to sell was that the property had a sentimental interest through having been left centuries ago by Benefactors whose memory they wished to honour. But when one came to enquire into the origin one found that, whilst the estate bore the Benefactor's name, he had in many cases left money by his will which he desired to have invested in land, and that the Governors, obeying his wishes, had bought an estate in the country.

The sentimental reason, therefore, vanished, and we were faced with the fact that, whilst the ownership of estates brought the owner social prestige, that was wasted on a corporate body like ourselves, whose sole object was to extend the benefits of the charity.

The second case is that of an agricultural estate of some 5500 acres in a southern county, the owner of which was in receipt of an income of barely £2000 a

year from it. The property realised a total of £193,000.
Allowing liberally for expenses, the purchase money,
invested at 5 per cent., would produce £9000 per
annum[1].

C. To the Industry

(1) State ownership of the land should tend to promote better farming. Where there is only one landlord
—the State—there would be no refuge for the man who
"runs" the land, and so the general standard of cultivation would tend to rise. As already shown, no other
form of tenure is calculated to deal so effectually with
under-farming (see p. 63).

(2) The improving tenant would not be hindered in
the practice of good husbandry through the neglect
of his neighbour farming under another landlord. It
happens too often nowadays that one man's land gets
waterlogged because his neighbour below has failed to
clean his ditches; or that his land is sown annually with
thistle seed blowing from his neighbour's fields. For
the past few years the State has been making grants in
aid of land drainage, and there is general agreement
amongst farmers that the work done has been of
very great benefit to the land. Notwithstanding this,
difficulties in dealing with private owners are not unknown; and it is obvious that the work would be
capable of very considerable extension if the State were
acting in its own interest and not by way of subventions
of individuals.

(3) The re-adjustment of farm boundaries would be
possible. At present many farms are badly laid out, so
that they cannot be worked with the maximum of
convenience and economy. Nor do all farms constitute

[1] Knight, Frank and Rutley, *op. cit.* pp. 10-11.

an "economic unit" for management. Some are too large for maximum production under one-man control; others are too small to give the tenant a fair chance of success; others, again, are badly balanced as regards the proportions of arable and grass land.

(4) Standardisation of systems of land tenure would be possible. As farms came on hand to be re-let a uniform tenancy agreement could be introduced in similar districts thus codifying the conditions of tenure.

(5) Coincidentally certain onerous customary payments on entry could be bought out by the State landlord which the private landowner cannot afford to do—as, for example, the "acclimatisation" value of sheep-flocks, and payments for "half-fallows" and "half-manures" which are required of the in-coming tenant in some districts.

(6) The provision of the necessary permanent equipment and the timely execution of repairs would be facilitated. The need for these is often recognised by the private landlord though it cannot be met by him owing to lack of resources. Taking a long view there is no doubt that expenditure on works of this nature, prudently incurred, will be remunerative in the form of additional rent; but even the owner able to ignore the fact that the immediate return is non-economic is often deterred from action, partly because he feels politically threatened, and so lacks confidence, and partly because recent legislation has hampered him, unfairly as he thinks, in obtaining either increases of rent or new tenants.

(7) Following on the foregoing, such matters as labourers' dwellings, schemes for water supply and drainage could be undertaken after consideration of the

needs of the locality as a whole—schemes which are at present impossible (quite apart from the question of finance) owing to the arbitrary division of the land into different ownerships. For example, the incidence of drainage rates would no longer be a matter of vital importance, and gigantic improvements such as the Ouse Valley Scheme could be carried through without the muddle which has accompanied it.

(8) The problem of credit would be solved, for the State could advance money to farmers on "chattel-mortgages" which are impossible under the present land tenure system.

(9) Co-operation and the organisation of farmers generally for industrial purposes would be more easily promoted.

(10) Advantage should result from the direct association of the new administrative department with the Ministry of Agriculture in the facility it would offer for the spread of information amongst farmers. The experience of the past thirty years has been that it is very difficult to bring the results of scientific investigation and discovery home to the individual practitioner, and the organisation recently set up by the Ministry for this purpose should receive an immediate stimulus from the administration of agricultural land by the State. It consists of a staff of advisory officers organised upon a county basis and working under a County Agricultural Committee. The County Land Agent should be *ex officio* a member of this Committee and this would secure a more intimate relationship between those concerned with the administration of land and those engaged in providing technical advice for farmers than that which exists at present

At this stage it is, perhaps, unnecessary to say any more about these proposals for the reform of agricultural land tenure. The justification claimed for them is first, that the old system admittedly has broken down; second, that the scheme of State-purchase outlined is one which would work. The principle upon which it is based, the recognition of undeveloped values without the attempt to assess them, safeguards the vendor against spoliation and the purchaser against attempting an impossible task.

It will be recognised that the scheme is intended only as a basis for discussion, but if it were to be accepted in principle it should not be difficult to arrive at agreement on points of detail. All parties in the State and all parties on the land are agreed that something will have to be done to deal with the situation; neither the industry itself nor the present Government have formulated schemes, so far, to cope with it. The suggestions of the Liberal Land Committee for the creation of Cultivating Tenancy follow a line opposed to the wishes of the great majority of English farmers —the last thing they desire is the opportunity to become landowners. Moreover, the basis upon which it is proposed to compensate the landlord is inequitable. He is to receive the "Fair Net Rent" of his property, but this sum may be reduced if the rate of wages, previously determined, should be so high as to make the payment of it impossible for the tenants. As a principle no one will quarrel with this attempt by the Committee to make the wages of labour a first charge on the industry, but that body seems to have failed completely to realise the peculiar position of agriculture when contrasted with other industries in this matter.

Speaking of the country generally the farmer's ability to pay wages, on any scale likely to be demanded, is quite independent of the amount of his rent. By altering his methods of farming so as to reduce the number of men employed he can adjust himself fairly quickly to wage-rates considerably higher than those prevailing, and unless the Committee are prepared, in some way, for the apparently impossible task of compelling farmers to adopt certain methods of farming so as to maintain certain standards of employment, the Fair Net Rent has not even a remote connection with the rate of wages. Thus, the suggestion that they are related could result only in an unfair valuation of the landlord's interest. Again, if prospective outgoings, such as higher wages, are to be reckoned against the landowner, is it not equitable that he should be entitled to prospective accretions of value? But the Committee contemplate nothing of the sort; on the contrary, they "emphasise the essential justice of providing that the values which accrue to agricultural land...should be enjoyed by the whole community, not by any individual who happens to own the land." There can be no essential justice in a scheme which contemplates saddling the landowner with the responsibility for losses whilst at the same time denying him the opportunity to make profits.

Other examples might be given of the inequitable treatment proposed for the landlord, but these must suffice. Unless the terms offered to him can be revised the Committee's scheme is doomed to failure, for there is no evidence of any volume of opinion in the country in favour of confiscation.

As to the Liberal Land Committee's proposals in regard to the farmer, enough has already been said to indicate his reluctance to function as landlord. Their scheme ties him to his holding, and charges him with a liability of unknown magnitude for the equipment and maintenance of it. Moreover his job is to farm; he has not been trained in the profession of land-agent and he has no knowledge of such technical matters as the planning and construction of buildings, surveying and levelling for land-drainage, schemes for water-supply, the principles of forestry, etc. The Committee contemplate supervision and pressure by the County Agricultural Authority to secure the execution of these works. But what degree of effective supervision can be exercised by a Committee, and what degree of pressure is likely to be applied by a body composed as it must be mainly of " Cultivating Tenants "? The application of the scheme would result in some cases in well-intentioned but inefficient attempts at the maintenance of holdings, and in others in the deliberate intention to annex the difference between the old rent as paid to the present landlords and the Fair Net Rent payable to the State.

The Labour Party aim at a control of the farmer's business which would be repugnant to him and so quite unworkable. It is suggested that the proposals set forth in the foregoing pages represent a reasonable compromise on widely diverging views, and that they are calculated to effect their purpose whilst, at the same time, introducing the smallest possible element of change into the present industrial order in agriculture.

INDEX

Printed in the United States
By Bookmasters